I0711728

PREFACE

O ver the last ten years, social media marketing has become an essential tool in the armory of brands and businesses of all sorts, with possibilities to build relationships, engage with clients, and boost sales like never before - and the stats back it up. A January 2018 survey by PewInternet revealed that 74% of adults in North America used social networking sites, including 82% of 30-49year-olds and 89% of 18-29 year-olds. In addition, research from social media analysts predicts that the growth of social commerce could make it a business worth $30 billion before the end of 2019. And in a Social Media poll carried in 2017, 91% of respondents said that social media marketing – worked on for at least 6 hours per week - increased exposure for their business. If you're not using social media at all, or your current strategy isn't working for you as well as you expected, now is the time to make a change. You are about to learn expert hints and tips to effectively market your business across all of the most popular social media platforms including Facebook, Twitter, Instagram, YouTube,

ARE YOU IN TIME TO MAKE A CHOICE?

choose the guide that helps you understand how, where and how many choices you can make!

If you're not using social media at all, or your current strategy isn't working for you as well as you expected,

now is the time to make a change.

You are about to learn expert hints and tips to effectively market your business

across all of the most popular social media platforms including...

Facebook-Twitter-Instagram-YouTube-Google+,Pinterest and more.

Written by Mary Joel.

TABLE OF CONTENTS

Google+, and Pinterest. Each chapter is grouped broadly into several sections including profile optimization, content strategy, and advice on paid advertising.

Victory in social media marketing comes from building effective and long-lasting relations with consumers and professional contacts, and sharing the variety of content and expertise that they will desire to share onwards to their colleagues, relatives , and co-workers. This strategy will assist to attract and keep loyal consumers and connections, and encourage brand ambassadors to sell your business for you – a complete reverse from the traditional marketing model! While this method is a world away from the way conventional marketing works, this open, two-way conversation is now what millions of users around the world expect from the companies and brands to whom they invest time and capital. Direct selling does have a position, but as you will learn, it is not the "beginning and center" where social media marketing is involved. I hope you find the following advice valuable, whether you are a complete social media novice or a savvy person looking for some more skillful tips to drive your company onto bigger and better things.

CHAPTER 1
INTRODUCTION

Business in today's day and time is dominated by consumers and their demands. People fancy to see referrals, reviews over Google search results , or a website before buying a product. To stand by the flow, we require to study what people say regarding us. You need to actively participate in associated communities to communicate and influence people. You need to interlace with social media to maintain your online status. Social media marketing is a necessity to target a wider client base and expand your company.

Social Media Marketing is the movement of driving website traffic through social media sites.

Tale of Social Media Marketing

Social Media appears to be a brand-new trend, but its origins stretch to the start of computer age. What we witness today is the outcome of centuries-old social media evolution. Usernets, which was begun in 1979, was the first progenitor of social media, and the course from Usernets to Facebook is a distant one. Usernets enabled users to post on newsgroups. It was succeeded by bulletin board systems (BBS) which permitted users to login and communicate. Following online services, internet relay chat reached into light which opened way to immediate messaging.

SMO Strategy for Business

A carefully executed Social Media Optimization (SMO) policy can give a great addition to your business. To draw greatest benefit out of Social Media, you require to set clear and distinct business aims and objectives. The following features are the backbone of any well-laid SMO procedure:

- Set assessable and achievable goals.

- Recognize you customers.

- Study market trends.

- Search more social networking stages.

- Reflect your appearance on all.

- Determine core topics associated to your

business. Utilize them in content.

- Set Social Engagement boundries.

- Organize your resource usage.

- Follow your results.

SMO − Key Concepts

- Aim for developing reputation by depicting yourself as a trusted source or business.

- Encourage more commitment and sharing.

- Be an entitled name in your business.

- Gear up creativity.

- Keep it social.

- Control over your media floors.

- Optimize every individual point that limits your efforts.

In the 90s, online dating sites and forums were on rise, which drove to the advancement of social networks. But they did not let users create friend lists. Six degrees started to overwhelm this feature. It enabled profile making and listing pears. It was obtained and shut down after operating for a decade. Blogging began in this phase, creating a excitement in social media. It is common even today. Other sites like BlackPlanet (African-American Social site) and MiGente (Latino) cropped up having preparation to develope profiles and add friends.

Modern social channels came into view post 2000. Apple originated its Friendster in 2002. It has millions of users. Hi5 and Linkedin were originated in 2003. Linkedin is a area for experts to reach out to one another. MySpace also introduced in 2003 and grew well known by 2006. Similarly Facebook was originated in 2004 and exceeded MySpace, Orkut, Multiply, etc., and is still growing. This decade also considered media sharing platforms like photobucket, flickr, youtube, instagram, etc., accompanying with news and bookmarking stages like Digg and Delicious.

Since 2000, Social Media has developed to horizon and is still expanding limitlessly. Accompanying with media sharing, many other openings that provide real-time updates were presented, for example, Twitter, Tumblr, etc. In 2007, Facebook started its marketing system.

Importance of Social Media

The influence of social media is undebatable. It is a strong channel of marketing − a game changer for any company. It presents us the flexibility to communicate at both personal as well as company levels.

Business owners can enhance search rankings, leads, sales, and traffic using research media. This can be performed at reduced marketing expenses. Besides business, it is a cool floor to connect with friends and loved ones.

Business Profile Creation

Design an impactful Business profile. Add a clear persona and proficiency statement of your business.

- Study competitors' company profile, examine their strong features, and add them to yours.

- Add noticeable features of your company that makes it noteable among others.

- Include the milestones accomplished by your company.

- Add address and other aspects.

- Enter data and statistics.

- List your famous vendors.

- Add some keywords to it to get marked by the web crawler.

Brand Awareness

Brand awareness is a point to which your brand name is recognized. Brand name solidifies customers' trust. So, it is essential that your brand name overshadows your commodities. Promoting the brand name assists your business develop and get over old-fashioned business state.

Social Media Marketing can assist you in stamping your business. It supports you increase your common profile as well. All you require is to

- Select right Social Media Channel for your company.

- Conclude a social content policy.

- Make a influential content plan.

- Engage in good communication with your clients to let them sense more connected.

- Keep track of all important metrics like possible reach, conversation share, connections, etc.

Social Engagement

Social Media Engagement is the method of reaching out to potential clients and interacting with them with Social Media. It is fundamentally done in order to bring attention towards a distinct product or a service. It is a two-way channel where a customer can share a good relation with the vendors.

To obtain optimum reach, you need to join with your audience. It can be a constant task. To get more out of less, you require to strategize your social media engagement measures.

- Use 'Social Channels' to reach out fans.

- Use Social Media stages to publish any event you are planning.

- Entertain Posts your fan is posting.

- Use Social Media Circles to engage in valuable and educational communications.

- Engage in Social Media groups.

- Measure your commitment level to trace your engagement efforts. It is fundamentally a ratio between the social platforms that you handle and the social stages that you do not use to engage. The higher is the level, the more powerful is your bonding with the public.

Viral Marketing

Any hot topic that is contagious is Viral Marketing. It is 'exposing an idea' for a reason. It is a message getting viral by transferring it from one to another with an purpose of promoting your business.

Social Media Viral Marketing is the usage of social media channels to spread any information for creating brand awareness. Viral marketing rate may differ on each level.

Examples of Viral Marketing

ALS Ice Bucket Challenge – ALS Association received increased media attention by soaking the whole world. Even celebrities and entrepreneurs participated in it.

Ashton Kutcher hits 1M – Ashton has been a seeding strategist who influenced his fans by an influencing message that went viral.

Hotmail went viral – Hotmail team placed a link 'Want a free email account? Sign-up for Hotmail today.' in the footer of any mail sent from a Hotmail account. It was a viral hit.

CHAPTER 2
BUILD A SOCIAL BUSINESS

What Is Social Business?

Social business—the use of social technologies as a formal element of business methods—revolves around learning how your consumers or stakeholders combine to your business and how you reshape your company to understand, accept, and innovate based on their engagement. Social business is about combining all of your business functions: customer support, marketing, the executive crew, and more. It implies doing this for the objective of creating collaborative innovation and commitment at meaningful, measurable levels tied clearly and directly to your organization's business goals.

Social Businesses Are Participative

Ultimately, social business is regarding cooperation with and by your customers and stakeholders in chase of an company that is strongly combined to them through participative and collaborative means. As a result, a social company is often better equipped to react to marketplace dynamics and ambitious opportunities than a traditionally organized and operated firm. This may happen through cooperation in a social community, a support or debate forum, or any of a variety of other social forms and contexts. The efforts beginning to the creation of a social business often begin with identifying or creating an opportunity for assistance with (or between) customers, workers, or stakeholders within association or similar social applications.

An essential feature to note here is that when social business practices are approached and implemented correctly, everyone wins. By bringing customers into the business, or directly involving stakeholders in the design and operation of the companies with which they are associated, a steady flow of ultimately constructive ideas emerges. One of the biggest misconceptions about social media and the Social Web as regards business commentary is that it's all negative, that the participants are all complainers and whiners. Not so.The fact is, unless your business strategy is to generate negative comments the Social Web is very likely presents significant opportunity for building your business and improving it over time.

Build Your Social Presence

Campaign-centric communities are not the focus of a social business program. If you discover yourself considering "campaign," you are either traveling for social-media-based marketing or conventional/digital marketing that is presented to "look like" social media. Beware: The center of social business—separate from social media marketing—is around the utilization of the Social Web to business in methods that are driven essentially through organic versus paid means and which are intended to benefit your business regularly versus sell commodities specifically.

Organic communities and Social Web projects built around a business are intended to exist independently of direct spending in marketing, with the possible sign of initial seeding. They are designed to notify the business, to connect it to its viewers, and to promote collaboration between customers and employees approaching the goal of improving the business, and to maintain this over time for the goal of driving superior business results. It is equally likely that the software and related infrastructure expenses of a social business program will be paid for through Operations or IT as through Marketing.

14

Again, this is not to state that there is no value in spend-driven societies . There is probably significant promotional value that arises out of measured fulfillment against marketing and advertising goals. It is to say that in addition to these varieties of marketing campaigns, social business plans are centered on focus business objectives and communicated through an appeal to the lifestyles, passion, and causes of clients. These types of programs are definitely put in place to encourage collaborative support. The collaboration that happens between customers and between workers is the source concentrates of social business.

So what is it that encourages organic growth and inserts the social technology-powered business on a road of its own? It comes back to the initial declaration that organic growth happens around lifestyles, passions, conditions, specific task-based utilities, and similar participant-centric projects and interests rather than brand, product, or service centered attributes. The prime challenge is therefore to align or combine the firm or company to an present community or to develop one around an actual lifestyle, passion, or cause that unites to the core business.

Business as a Social Participant

People gather around a given interest, cause, or lifestyle in pursuit of a sense of collective experience. Important to understand is that they are often motivated by an apparent desire to talk about a brand, product, or service experience with each other, relating this to what they have in common. What they have in common may in part be that brand, product, or service, but it is generally also something deeper. Apple products—and the following they have created—are a great example of this: Apple owners are seemingly connected by Apple products, but in a deeper sense they are connected by the ethos of Apple and the smart, independent lifestyle associated with the brand.

For LEGO enthusiasts—and in particular adult LEGO enthusiasts— there is a gathering that occurs on LUGNET.com along with a variety of other fan-created websites, forums, and blogs. Conversations appear to revolve around LEGO products, but in reality the higher calling is the shared passion for creation, which LEGO (as a product) facilitates. While LEGO creation may bring members to the community, and while it may be the common thread that unites a seemingly disparate group, the camaraderie is what keeps members together

16

years upon years. A business or organization is itself in many respects a social place. In much the same way, the social business is a place where employees and customers gather together around a common purpose of creating the products and services that define—and are often subsequently defined by—the brand and its higher purpose. Employees and customers, together through collaboration, create the experiences they want: Together they are responsible for the business. When the conversations that result are a reflection of this shared interest of both customers and employees, the conversations themselves are very likely to be powerful expressions that carry the business or organization forward.

This kind of end result—an expressed passion around a brand, product, or service—is associated with the higher stages of engagement. Beyond consumption of content, engagement in the form of curation of community interaction, creation of content and collaboration between participants are the activities leading to advocacy. Consider the role that collaboration plays in contributing to the sense of ownership as a result of the combined efforts of employees and customers, participating together in the creation of a shared outcome. This sense of joint ownership, however subtly it may be expressed, is in fact a reasonable and even required customer sentiment that once and for all "cuts through the clutter."

Collaborate

Collaboration—sitting atop the engagement process—is the defining expression of measurable engagement. Marketers often speak of engagement: For example, one might focus on time spent on a page, or the number of retries a customer is willing to undergo before meeting with success. Measures such as "returning visitors," connected to concepts such as "loyalty" are also used as surrogates for engagement. While all of these have value within the discipline of marketing—and most certainly have a role in establishing efficacy of brand and promotional communications over a period of time—they do not in and of themselves provide a quantitative basis for the stronger notions of engagement as defined in the social business context. The direct observation of collaboration does.

Collaboration between community members, between employees, or between a fi rm and its representatives comes about when both parties in the transaction see a value in completing the transaction, often repeatedly. The output of collaborative processes—the number of jointly developed solutions advanced in an expert's community, for example—is directly measurable. Think about counting the number of collaborative processes that lead to a solution, or the number of shared results. Each is an indicator of the respective participant's willingness to put effort into such processes. In this sense, the quantitative assessment of collaboration becomes a very robust indicator for the relative strength of the engagement process.

Participation

Participation is likely one of the easiest metrics to capture and track. Indicators of participation can be gathered from existing measures—content creation, curation, and the number of reviews, comments, and posts—and can then be used to assess the overall levels of interest and activity within online communities.

At the most basic level, as with any online interaction, the activity itself can be tracked. Accessing a page, submitting a form, downloading a file and similar content measures provide a well-understood framework for measurement. However, given the existence of profiles (explored more in the next section) and the behaviors associated with curation—rating, ranking, etc.—much more interesting and useful metrics can be established and used to create very robust measures of participation.

As another aspect of participation and its direct measurement, consider "pointbased" social community reputation systems. Participants in a support community are very often rewarded through increasing social rank based on contribution to the community. Upon joining, you may be assigned the rank of "newbie" and then over time earn your way to "expert" status as you contribute and gain the votes of others in the community as they curate your contributions. At some level, there is a basic point system that is translating individual actions within the community into personal reputations: it may be visible, or it may be buried in the inner working of the community's reputation management system. Either way, it's there and can tapped as a source of metrics. When participants do something beneficial, they earn a point. When they do something that offends the community they might lose a point. Track both and you've got a solid assessment of participation.

In a thoughtful analysis using tested techniques applied in a novel manner, social media strategist Bud

Caddell points out a very straightforward method for calculating the relative distribution for participation and thereby gaining quantitative insight into the role of community influencers. Bud's method—simplified—is based on a statistical approach to tracking the spread in variance based on ratings points over time. Communities that have high variance are being influenced by a relatively small number of people compared with those with lesser variance. This is important because over time what is generally desirable is a more equitable distribution of participative effort—lower variance—across the community.

CHAPTER 3

BEFORE YOU BEGIN:

KEY CONSIDERATIONS FOR

ALL SOCIAL

MEDIA MARKETING

Peer stress, victory stories in the media and overall hype tell today's business owners that having a presence on social media is essential. That's not to say a company couldn't do great without utilizing social networking, but they'd surely be missing out on a myriad of possibilities to build and grow.However, one of the greatest mistakes that a brand can make is to jump into social media marketing with no real hint of what they are going to do with it; only the dim hope it will somehow make their fortune. While there is a likelihood that you get really lucky, in most instances this kind of unplanned passageway will lead to unrealistic goal-setting, poor results, a huge loss of time, and ultimately a defeatist approach that puts you off the idea of social media marketing altogether.To ensure that this doesn't occur to you – and to give you the best possibility of success - I urge you to understand the key factors for social media marketing described below. By the conclusion of this topic, you will have a great knowledge of what kind of approach works for company on social media, and how to take your energies in a well-planned, logical way.

Decide which social networks will operate best for you

Unless you are a large company with the financial resources to push full speed ahead into every conceivably viable social platform, possibilities are you are better to concentrate on one or two "core" social networks first. It's more useful to excel on a couple of social networks than be standard on 5 or 6, and while social media is free, your time is important. Indeed, depending on the nature of business you run,not every social media section is going to entertain your marketing, your audience, or what you are striving to achieve. To help you choose where to begin, identify which social networks your target viewers already "hangs out" or use consumer personas and research of social network demographics to judge where you will best be received.

Joining Facebook and Twitter is often a given for brands just due to their sheer size and importance, but more "niche" societies with their own unique attributes - still with hundreds of millions of users, mind you -like Instagram, or LinkedIn, might be where you discover you can make an influence more successfully. You will discover all about what each appropriate social network brings to the table as they are included in the chapters to come, but to start off, try with a couple of social networks where you can spend some important time, track your progress, and then either build on your successes with them, or steadily begin to try with other stages on which you might have extra (or better) victory.

Define and assess your goals

Before you begin posting content to social media, it is beneficial to define the guiding

themes and overall aims of your policy, as these will assist you shape the direction

you methord what may well display the linchpin in your marketing tool.

I'm a fan of the clever technique for generating actionable social media objects.

Here's a breakdown, hopefully they'll assist you too:

Specific: Be specific in what you desire to achieve. Do you want to raise

consciousness of your brand? Enhance sales? Enhance customer service? Encourage

loyalty?

Measurable: How will you recognize that your goal has been accomplished? What

analytics tools will you utilize to track your development?

Achievable: Is your goal sensible? When you are just beginning off, don't aim too

big at the chance of being deflated if you don't hit your predicted goal; getting

really skilled at all this stuff (particularly if you are addressing social media

marketing sincerely for the first time) takes a some time.

Relevant: Is your goal aligned with your organization's mission, vision and values?

Time Specific: When do you want to have achieved

the goal by? To add a focus

to your marketing, attach to one overarching aim at a time, e.g. "I want to

enhance traffic to my website by 15% in the following 3 months".

For instance, if you are a shoe store owner and you regularly sell 20 pairs of

footwear a day, why not aim to utilize social media to help you sell 30 per day? After a good significance of time (at least a few months), assess where you are by utilizing

analytics tools, social insights (likes, followers, comments), and other metrics to

assist you track and mark your activity - you will find lots more knowledge on

these quickly.

Perform an audit to assist shape your content strategy

Carrying out an inspection is one of the best ways to get an idea of the kind of social media content strategy that will resonate with your viewers, and a great way to decide upon what you desire to post to your viewers. Take time to recognize your viewers's needs, wants, and curiosities on social media - question yourself what obstacles you can assist them overcome, what problems you can answer, what type of content they favor (e.g. text, picture, graphics, video), and when they are very likely to be around to witness it. Tools like SEM Rush and Genuine Social Metrics are two successful paid options if you desire to dig right down into the features, but you need not pay a penny to get a good, overall idea... particularly if you use your competition to assist you out! First, identify your rivals (you'll presumably know them already, but a single google search will tell you), then hit their websites and social accounts for a nose around. Make records on how often your competitors publish blogs and standing updates on social media, and which content appears to perform most suitable for them depending on the number of likes, comments,and shares. You can obtain further insight by recognizing how much of this content appears to be real versus shared from other origins, and what the themes and tone of voice practiced are like. Use the knowledge you gather to mirror prosperous types of content in your own social media plan, but also to recognize gaps and opportunities where you can do great.

Plan leading with a social media content schedule

One of the most difficult tests challenging brands on social media is to consistently advertise high quality content for their followers. A company's social media appearance that appears deserted is the digital equivalent of switching your lights off. Because you're not updating online, fans will assume that you are going out of business,even if the contrary is true. Since it is this flexibility that can really assist to boost levels of commitment (by enabling fans to anticipate your next post) and promote a stronger relationship with your viewers (who will come back for more), one of the greatest ways to assist get it right is by organizing a social media content schedule. An editorial schedule will allow you to design your activity for weeks - or even months - in advance.

This foresight will enable you to create seasonal themes into your updates, and prevent you from posting sub-par material just because you require to publish something. As well as designing for the big holidays like Eid and Christmas, you will also be capable to map out a procedure for "mini holidays" like July 4th or Valentine's Day, events where fans are actively seeking on social media for sales, discounts, advice, etc. The capability to browse a social content schedule regularly will also provide you with away to step back from day-to-day posting and reaffirm your more comprehensive strategy. Of course, continous posting to social media yet has a place, but for the base of your strategy, a content schedule is highly suggested. One simple way to plan a content plan (that can be used to populate your schedule and prevent yourself from growing overwhelmed) is to generate a daily theme over your social networks. For instance: sharing a new blog post on Monday,asking a question on Tuesday, an infographic on Wednesday, a quote on Thursday, etc.

Re-purpose content across social media

It is worth stressing that something that might be scattered as one piece of content in the real life (a press release, say), can be marketed as 4 or 5content pieces for social media: blog regarding it, tweet, create a video, share on Instagram. This is a fabulous strategy for making the most utmost of your content development, especially if you are tied for time or low on supplies.

Drop old-style communication techniques and get social – find and establish your social voice

Successful social media policy requires just that - a social strategy. Traditional marketing methods like TV and newspaper publicity worked because the direction of conversation could only go in 1 direction (from brand to user)with little possibility for reply, but social media suggests that this is no longer the case. Now that a two-way conversation is firmly planted and your brand is under the attention 24/7, you must oppose the urge to talk at people, and change your tone of voice and contact methods to join with them on a human level -conversing to them in a personable manner and hearing with intent, rather than just listening and doing nothing regarding it.

This lesson concerns the same whether you are a small company operating a handful of people, a multi-national company with thousands of workers, the owner of a "fun" business like a karaoke bar, or something more "serious" like a finance company. companies that represent their social view (and strive to preserve it in all of their social communications) can cut within the noise and deliver a clear communication that, ultimately, will deliver more enhanced results. There are moments
30

where something like the old-school design of direct promotion is useful, but need to spend the preponderance of your time being much more selfless, even going out of your way to make individual customers feel special as a way to create a good feeling regarding your product or service that moves way beyond that one indvidual.

Humanize your brand and be emotive

People utilize social media to join with other people, so lower your barriers and display followers the authentic you, and the individuals behind your company' logo; be clear, open, and genuine in all of your contact – authenticity often means being a little bit more open about what your business might traditionally share with customers, but there's a fine line – if you're consistently sharing posts about internal conflicts or your love life, that line has probably been crossed! establish your unique voice, show a sense of humor, use everyday language, etc. And if being authentic endears consumers to you, then they will be more likely to want to engage with your content, share it on to others, and support you financially when the time comes to buy, by choosing you over another brand who they have no connection with. Rather than attempting to manipulate fans into buying products or service, showcasing you and your company's true values and character will go a long way to establishing you separate from your rivals.While all of this advice applies to your text interactions and tone of voice, human, emotional connections are similarly important in visual content.

Studies

Register that images of individuals (as compared to inanimate objects) - particularly

those smiling and getting eye contact with the observer - can assist to drive exchange rates. Even if the commodity you are selling is intangible, e.g. data or financial services, you should yet try to include individual faces into at least some of your pictures, whether they be of you, your consumers, or simply people in stock pictures. On a similar note – and a powerful pairing to text alone – are emoticons. A study by Amex Open found that utilizing emoticons in status updates improved comments by an aggregate of 33%, while a separate research by Buddy Media found that posts with emoticons took on average 57% more likes, 33% greater amount of comments and 33% and greater number of shares. Perhaps more notable is that various social sites – Twitter, Instagram, and Facebook added - all support the use of Emoji – fully -drawn, expressive emojies and ideograms that have fast convert a global language all of their own, can combine a whole new layer of fun and emotion to your status updates. In a 2015 report, Instagram discovered that nearly 50 percent of all titles and comments had at least one Emoji.

Don't over-promote: build relationships and provide value

The large majority of social media users do not visit Facebook, Twitter, Pinterest, et. to be delivered the hard sell by businesses; they utilize them to communicate with family and colleagues, and to be inspired. If they do "like" or "follow" companies on social media, they usually do so on a whim (think regarding the number you "like" or"comments"), and all but the most enthusiastic followers won't care to see every individual post you upload (in fact, it is foolish to think that you can even make it appear without using money). Therefore, it is your responsibility to persuade people to fancy having your company as something that is a big chunk of their everyday lives, and proceed to earn your place - do not see it as a right, view it as a privilege. You do this by developing trusting and loyal connections, by being friendly, sharing excellent content, assisting individuals with client service issues (with the odd promotional post in within, of course... which if the foundation of your strategy is up to scratch, your audience really should not care).

Ultimately, with social media content in brain, adjust your mindset from "what can we give you?" to "what can we do to assist you?", because in terms of selecting to follow a company on social media, your followers will sure be interrogating "what's in it for me?" With match up and organic (non-paid) limit (the amount of people who see your content) at an all-time low, it is necessary that the content you post touches individual on a private and passionate level. Some of the most important emotional triggers are fun, fear, anger, and even narcissism (stuff that, by distribution, makes the individual look good in front on their peers on social media).

Once you get into your stride, one helpful exercise to assist you keep on record is as follows: from time to time, pause and take a look at your previous 10 social media posts and question yourself this: "What value am I presenting and what direction am I serving?" If you can not clearly determine the answer to this question, you should consider carefully regarding improving your approach to better reach viewers who are now more intelligent and savvier than ever before; people who easily view past weak content or an over-sale information. Just similar in the real world, social media members will resonate more with a name that they can admire and trust, much more than one whose single mission seems to be to inspire them to open their wallets at every occasion. To reemphasize the point I made before, you should strive to become a seamless member of their supposed social media experience, not a jarring factor that they desire to skip past. All of this great work will build a assertive image around your company and slowly convert into sales.

Consistently post high quality content

First and foremost, do not start a presence on a social media outlets, post for a few weeks, and then let its activity fit in! For largest social networks, one, two or three updates per day is a good aim, but at a minimum , you should upload at least a some of times a week so that your content stays to appear in the news feeds of your most committed fans. To single out Facebook as an instance of a social network that a vast majority of companies use, here's some more comprehensive prospect to describe why persistence is so essential: When someone goes through their Facebook News Feed, there are an aggregate of 1,500 possible posts – created according to the site's complex algorithm - that they can be displayed at any given time, from friends, Pages, groups, etc. Add the fact that around half of users do not check Facebook each day (and, of those that do, they only skim for around 30-60 minutes in whole), the chances of all of your posts being viewed and employed with in among all of that competition, falls considerably. In reality with out paid advertising (which we will look at later), Facebook makes it almost impossible for all of your followers to see all of your posts, and brands must now work harder than ever to eek as much free, organic reach out of their Facebook activity as possible. Facebook still offers businesses a ton of potential, but it is no longer as simple as it once was.

In addition to the earlier, in order to ensure that as many individuals as possible view the content you post (whether on the social network it was originally posted or if shared elsewhere), it must be top quality, i.e. the sort of entertaining, effective, inspirational, valuable

36

stuff that somebody will like, comment, click (if a link is included) and share. In fact, in August 2013 - in an attempt to filter News Feeds to display only "high quality" content from brands - Facebook surveyed thousands of users on what they regarded as "high quality" content, folded the answers into its machine learning system and integrated it all with a master algorithm. This algorithm considers "over a thousand different factors," including the quality of a business Page's other content and the level of completion of its profile when determining whether a post is "high quality" enough to be broadcast in the News Feed to its fullest potential. Most people and companies have a limited of "go-to" sources, either in their preferences or subconscious – websites and social forms that they routinely receive from (you presumably have your own, in fact). This selection ensures them consistently helpful content they can share with their associates and followers, and your plan should be to grow as one of these trusted references.

The bottom line is that the extra consistently involved a consumer is with your posts on social media material - liking, commenting, sharing - the highly likely they are to remain to do so in future. And in the matter of Facebook, assertive communication like this will guarantee that your posts are to continue to emerge in their News Feed for future engagement shots. To connect to Facebook one more time, its News Feed Algorithm filters material into persons' feeds according to what it thinks is most suitable to them, so if a follower never views posts from you (because you are inactive), overlooks your posts for a extended period of time because they are not appealing enough (or, worse, has used the option to hide them), they will die from that person's News Feed and you may find it hard to get them back in there without paying for the opportunity.

Note: With natural ability on Facebook and other social networks at an all-time low, it may seem that the most suitable solution to obtain exposure for your content is to post especially frequently. However, in some means this approach is really counter-natural. Not even your most enthusiastic fans will enjoy being regularly flooded by posts from you, and by reducing the pressure of demanding to produce a speedy stream of top rank content day in, day out, you give more time to make sure that what you do issue is as great as it can be - material that will collect the most commitment from fans. In addition, if you change the time spent on "excess" content for promoting "core" material with a few advertisement dollars, you increase the amount of unique fans who see these posts and - if they interlace with a like, comment, or share - they are more suitable (at least in the case of facebook) to feed the next one wholly in the News Feed.

Which kind of posts get the greatest engagement?

One of the big discussions between social media marketers is whether text, picture, video, links, or other post samples are the most efficient in reaching viewers and encouraging them to communicate. The truth is that nobody can say you for sure - social networks are forever squeezing their algorithms, forcing companies to play catch-up - and at the conclusion of the day, it very much depends on what your specific data communicates to you is running best. For instance, back in 2012 Facebook was telling companies that posts that carry a photo album, image or video produce about 180%, 120% and 100% more commitment respectively than text posts alone, but what method is that potential for commitment if you see that your text posts at any provided point in time happen to transfer 5x the volume of people than when you use pictures? And in January 2014, Facebook announced that link-share posts (those that create an automatic picture thumbnail when a news article or website address is distributed within a status update) should be chosen because "when people view more text status updates on Facebook they communicate more status updates themselves." My advice is to withstand the appeal to recklessly chase trends, fads, or "no guarantee" tricks that guarantee to deliver high levels of commitment! Instead, utilize them as a guide but constantly concentrate on providing awesome, valuable material first. Continue to test and squeeze with a close eye on your own statistics, and keep adjusting to push on with what is running best for you (not everybody else) at any given moment.

Do not get hung up on reach; concentrate on creating faithful, passionate followers and meaningful connections

As you now know, fierce rivalry between individuals, companies and the process social networks' algorithms operate, indicates that not all of your followers will see your posts in their news feeds when you distribute them, and by their own acknowledgment, sites like Facebook recognize that this situation is only going to get even bad as more and more companies enter the conflict. Therefore, you need to imagine less regarding chasing "likes", follower amounts, and post limit - as these things (although having some attraction and merit, particularly if they are from and transferring a target, high quality public) can often be unpredictable. Instead, focus more on producing great material that will develop you a loyal audience who love what you do (giving it via post likes, comments, sharing your content, and ultimately through sales), therein helping more people to spend in your cause. This works not just for Facebook, but every social media. I would say if you are getting anyplace near 10% stretch to all of your followers without paid advertising, you are doing remarkably well.

Social media sucks up time

Social media is now an indispensable marketing and PR tool, and should be considered thoughtfully. If you ask an current employee to take over charge for your social media output, do not anticipate them to be able to do it as well as their current job. If you're going the whole hog, expect it to take up at least 12-15 hours a week to design, create, and calendar content, test results, as well as engaging with customers. Consider hiring somebody into the position of Social Media Administrator full time. Alternatively, outsource your project to a local specialist marketing company, experts who can assist you hit the ground running. If you do, guarantee that they recognize your brand, marketing goals, and address your consumer's voice.

Create a social media policy, make workers ambassadors

A clear, company-wide social media strategy will clarify the concerns of staff specifying of your company on social media and enable them to positively promote your company, assisting to make you a more socially active company. To prepare the data you require, consult with the key influencers in your industry, adhere to state and federal laws and regulations, collect feedback from your workers, and outline guidelines regarding usage of social media (whether mentioning your company or not), both within and beyond working hours. Try to compile the most significant points in a report no longer than one or two pages (otherwise it might not be read and leave you exposed to problems in the future), and highlight the advantages that effective usage of social media can lead to the company as a whole. Employees require to feel certain about social sharing guidelines to be great brand ambassadors, so make writing company-related situations easy by - for instance - inventing a hashtag associated to life at your company, and encourage them to take photographs and share updates utilizing it. The person in command of social media content, of course, should understand the policy completely.

Social media marketing is not free; experiment with paid advertisements

Many years ago, social media marketing was viewed as a golden opportunity to reach and promote to customers for free. In certain aspects, this was true. Now, however, with greater competition and a more astute audience, paid promotion across is all-but necessary. That is not to say you can not still achieve splendid results without paying a penny, but even a simple figure, filled well (such as $5 per workday on highly targeted Facebook advertisements), can noticeably increase a company's success. The solution to a lot of thriving social media promotion are advertisements that combination into a a consumer's exposure of the site or app on which they seem, mirroring the tone and publishing style of the public - as with non-paid content, think seamless instead of disruptive.

Above all, enjoy the ride; build powerful, meaningful connections

The stronger someone introduces with your company on social media, the more likely they will remember you and pass the assertive word on to their colleagues and family. Be regular , present, real and authentic in all of your message if you want to encourage genuine communication with customers on a slow and steady path to building loyalty, sales and company's advocates for life.

CHAPTER 4

FACEBOOK TIPS:MARKETING STRATEGY YOU WILL LIKE AND SHARE

F acebook is the most used social media in the world, with well over one billion users on computer and mobile. As the ruler of social networks, your target audience is almost guaranteed to be there. Use these tips to create, brand and market your company on Facebook, as well as a mass a following of highly interested consumers.

Facebook Business Page Setup Strategy

Before you jump in and begin uploading on Facebook, it needs to take some time to lay solid grounds to assist get your company attendance set up properly, and in a place to move fans when they discover you. Let's get started on the path to making your small corner of Facebook a purpose that people will revisit regularly.

Create a Facebook Page, not a individual's profile

When you register to Facebook, you are allocated a Personal Timeline by default. Particular Timelines, seldom mentioned to as profiles, are created for individual, non-commercial usage. For your company to take benefit of everything Facebook marketing has to contribute, you need to design a separate Facebook Page. Facebook Pages look comparable to personal Timelines, but present unique tools for companies like analytics, custom tabs to host business-related data, and marketing tools. Pages do not need separate Facebook accounts and do not have separate login data from Timelines. You can generate a Facebook Page in one of three ways: by seeking 'Create A Page' in the exploration bar at the top of the website, by clicking the 'Create A Page' badge at the top of any present Facebook Page.

Keep your Facebook Page name compact; get it true the first time!

If at all feasible, try to hold your Facebook Page name compact, as this will assist if you go on to build Facebook advertisements, where the headline area in the advert (usually the name of your Page) is restricted to just 25 characters. You can only modify the name of a Facebook Page manually if it has less than 200 likes, so make certain you are happy with yours early on. If you are not satisfied with your Page name and it qualifies to be substituted, go to the "About" tab positioned underneath your Page's cover photo. Click "Edit" next to the Name section and save. Changing your Page's name does not influence its username or Page web address (explained below).

Get a custom Facebook web address for your Facebook Page

Set up a display URL for your Facebook Page (available when you gain 25 likes),ideally named after your brand. This will make it much more comfortable for you to inform people how to locate your Facebook Page. Think about it thoroughly, as you will only be able to modify this URL once in futurity (via the "About" tab), otherwise you will have to erase your Page and start over - not great if you've developed a big fan base! To communicate the 25-fan door quickly, invite your e-mail connections and current Facebook friends - a society of people who already care regarding you and your company - to visit and "Like" your Page, via the "Promote" drop-down list at the top of your Facebook Page.

Fill in business information correctly and in detail

Fill in as much of your company details as feasible in the About segment of your Facebook Page, including address, contact details, merchandise information, website (add multiple URLs by parting them with commas in the website box), and links to other social accounts. Putting the work into populating these segments makes your Page helpful to consumers who can see all of your necessary data in one place, and the keyword-rich blurb is also great for search engine optimization (SEO), as the text in your About section is arranged by Google. Restaurant owner and chosen Restaurant/Cafe as your Page's kind? Make sure you add the types of meals you serve, and also upload your menu as a PDF for consumers to browse, or if you're in the U.S. or Canada, you can also add a menu through Single Platform.

Note: Depending on how your Page is categorized, sometimes the first-viewed bit of the About section displays differently on the Facebook mobile app than it does to desktop viewers. For some mobile users, it will show your Short Description, others your Mission, and others still, a portion of your full Company Description. With this in head, it may be smart to amend all of these sections to begin with your website URL so that you can guarantee that is always the first thing that mobile users see.

Confirm your Page and get an authentic check mark on your cover picture

If your business has a real world address, Facebook allows you to verify your Page to adorn its cover photo with an official grey check mark - similar to the blue one given to celebrities and other public figures. To confirm your Page, view your Page Settings and choose Verify Page under the General menu. You will require to confirm your business-representative state via a telephone call to a publicly listed number for your business, or otherwise upload an official document, e.g. business phone or utility bill, business license, business tax file, etc. Verified Pages display higher in search results and reveal people at a glance that you are the genuine brand Page for your company on Facebook, so it is well worth doing.

Create a remarkable cover photo and attach a call-to-action switch

Facebook Page cover pictures can be seen by anyone on Facebook, so utilize the space to efficiently communicate your brand or information in one simple, high quality, picture. The ideal size is 851 × 315 pixels - any smaller and Facebook will automatically stretch the image, making it appear blurry. Ideas for cover photos incorporate one powerful image that conveys who you are and what you do, a collage of your commodities, highlighting an ongoing offer, or featuring a picture or testimonial presented by one of your own followers - the latter will really "wow" your consumer and hopefully they will publish the word to their fellows. Keep users interested by periodically updating your cover photo and profile pic - once per month is a good target to aim for, but a seasonal change is popular amongst companies, too.

Add a call to action, stretches and links in the cover pattern and description. In December 2014, Facebook declared the roll out of solid, clickable call-to-action keys that can be attached to cover photos, including "Book Now", "Contact Us," "Use Application. Designed as a means to bring your company' most important purpose to the forefront of your Facebook presence, call-to-action buttons can be connected to any address on or off Facebook.

Design Facebook Page custom tabs to advertise your services

Custom tabs display in the "Apps" section on the left-hand side of your Facebook Page and are great little hub for things like promoting your products and services, most popular blog posts (Networked Blogs is a good choice), for hosting contests, sharing customer testimonials, inviting people to "Like" your Page to be informed of exclusive news and promotions in their News Feeds, or supporting people to sign up to your e-mail list. Just search for a distinct kind of app in Facebook's search bar, e.g. "contest app" and possibilities are it will be automatically proposed to you and can be installed in just a few clicks. Apps can also be utilized to cross-promote your other social accounts like Pinterest, Instagram, YouTube, Twitter, etc. One of the most reliable methods to populate custom tabs to look exactly as you fancy (with branded layout, links, etc.) is with the free of cost Static HTML iframe app. As an instance, I used the Static HTML app to develop a 'Welcome' tab, which encourages consumers to "Like" my page for free social media video tutorial updates, and gives notice about my book, with a clickable link to buy it at Amazon. To get started, simply discover and install the Static HTML iframe application via the Facebook's search bar.

Provide to mobile consumers by promoting check-ins, and utilizing Place Tips

When a user sees your Page and business knowledge on the Facebook mobile application, they'll also be given information like which of their mates have viewed and checked in, and whether they or the broader Facebook community have recommended you with pictures, star ratings and reviews on show. Understanding this, it pays to support people to "check-in" if you have a real-life place. Display notices in notable areas of your company, such as the entrance, receipts and point of sale, to urge customers to get out their smartphones, check-in and notify their friends of where they are, boosting them to visit too. When a review is left for a company, a status update is produced that goes out to the News Feed of that clients' friends, along with the company' cover and profile photo and its star evaluation.

If a client is already at your place and opens the Facebook app, Place Tips get into play. Place Tips utilizes Wi-Fi, GPS, and Bluetooth (for the latter, you can use for a Bluetooth "beacon" to beam your data to automatically show viewers more information regarding your company, including the aforementioned surveys, photos, check-ins, etc. In extension, it will inspire people to check-in and like your Page and, via the About segment of your profile, you can specify a custom Welcome Note to greet clients to your establishment - perhaps give them a heads-up on promotions and discounts too!

Facebook Marketing Basics

Now that your Facebook Page is looking fabulous and you are encouraging people to visit it, let's explore some ways that you can make the most effective use of the platform, in conjunction with the content strategy ideas.

Pin eminent posts

Facebook enables you to pin a single post to the top of your Page's timeline for up to a week. Utilize this to highlight valuable content, and make it more noticeable to followers who visit your Page. All new status updates will seem below the pinned post until it is unpinned (or a week elapses), whereupon it will come into its original chronological place. After creating a post, hover over it till the pencil icon arrives, click it and choose 'Pin to Top'. In special, posts to consider pinning include special messages, contents, discounts, etc.

Boost communication with Facebook-embedded posts

In August 2013, Facebook rolled out the capability to embed personal account or Page posts into an outer website. Utilize embedded posts to lift conversations from your Facebook Page to help inspire and boost interaction with your statuses in places away from the site, like as part of a blog post, or even in an email newsletter as a way to encourage browsers to your Page. As long as the status you update, anybody can embed it from your Facebook Page or re-embed them from wherever else it appears, which - if your status is actually shareable - could give your Page and content a lot of publicity. Embedded posts even insert keys for observers to "Like, comment, and share the post", and a button to "Like" your page to get notified.

How to embed a Facebook post

- Move over the post you want to embed, left-click on the sign that arises, and select "Embed Post".

- Copy the code that arises and paste it as HTML on your site or blog.

Re-post top cut content, but do not be spammy regarding it

As not everyone reviews their Facebook News Feed all day each day, and only a tiny proportion of your followers will see your material first time around, if you have a great article or link to share, post it numerous times as a way for as numerous of your followers to see it as possible. However, make a collective effort to share the data under various guises, e.g., different expression in the text, an image with a link, a link share post, etc. Although picture-with-a-link posts are worth testing with, traditional link share posts come several often recommended because they reveal the way that the common person uses Facebook... when did you last see a colleague sharing a link with an uploaded image? Facebook will punish your reach if you publish the specific same status over and again, as it has discovered people react adversly to "copy and paste" posts.

Encourage clicks through call-to-actions but avoid "click-baiting"

To promote higher click-through measures from Facebook and other social media to your site and blog, being explicit about what you desire your consumers to do using a definite call to action is usually a good bet, e.g. "Click here for more data [your link]". Sometimes that little push can execute all the distinction between a thriving status and one that falls without a trace.

Guarantee views with "Get All Announcements" and "See First" approach

One tactic that can be utilized to all-but ensure that followers see all of your Page's content is to prepare them to subscribe to the "Get Notifications" and "See First" choices, found in a drop-down menu when moving their cursor over the "Liked" and "Following" switch underneath your Page's cover photo. With this chosen, every time you post a new status update, the followers in question will be notified with a notification under the blue "globe" icon in the status bar of their Facebook profiles, and your new material will appear at the top of that users' News Feed respectively. These applications are properly conveyed through a status update with a screen grasp of the menu, to show the exact action that you want them to take. Whether or not you are pleased with asking at the risk of appearing pushy is up to you, and you should judge it based on the power of the relationship you have with your viewers. If you do determine to do it, I would not force it upon followers very often, particularly as they are unlikely to be right on your Page when they see your instructions appear, and even more unlikely to click through and carry it out.

Optimize blog photographs to make an impression on Facebook

In September 2013, Facebook launched a notable

increase to the size that thumbnail images from linked articles surface in the News Feed. When you update a status including a link, Facebook will automatically pick an picture from the article, and as long as it is of satisfactory size, that image will demonstrate at full width on your Page and in News Feeds, with the blog title and blurb under it. In specific terms, for a linked article's picture to perform at full width on Facebook, the width of the image requires to be 1.91 times its height. Facebook advises an image that is at least 1200×630 pixels, which, honestly, isn't realistic for most bloggers. Rather, aim to produce blog posts that include at least one image that is 600×315 pixels (even if it a picture that is uploaded large, but contracted to fit your blog's formatting style), as this is the smallest size that Facebook needs for any linked article's image to present at full width in any location on all devices - desktop, mobile, or tablet. If your connected article's chosen image is below 600×315 pixels, Facebook will automatically resize it much smaller.

Switch between YouTube and Facebook-uploaded video

The rise of video content on Facebook has altered the

landscape of the social network, and it is only going to get more significant. In many instances, it pays to upload appealing video content straight to the site, rather than, for instance, sharing a YouTube link. This is because original Facebook video is provided a more favorable ride in words of reach (but keep an focus on your analytics to see how everything go). If the video is "evergreen" in character (i.e. it'll still as relevant in the future as it is now) why post the video twice - once by uploading straight to Facebook, and at a succeeding date via a shared YouTube link? Policies to maximize the result of videos uploaded to Facebook:

- Videos uploaded to Facebook play automatically – and are muted with no audio - within the News Feed. With this in mind, think how you will hook your followers into viewing your clip (and turn the sound on) from the very first frame – catching someone's eye with movement in the first 2-3 seconds is one way to do this, or if a person is seen talking in front of camera, fans who are interested will click to hear what's being said.

- Manage videos into playlists via the Video tab on your page (to encourage increased watch time), and select one video to Feature.The

Featured video will surface in prime position below the "About"segment in the sidebar of your Page - a big opportunity for an opening video to your company, or to highlight a current promotion.

- Tag people who feature in your videos, add descriptive labels, and select the best thumbnail available in the menu that appears after the file has been uploaded (or upload your own custom image). And don't forget to grab the video embed code to include in a blog post on your website to encourage more exposure and interaction – choose between embedding the whole status update, or just the video player itself for a cleaner look.

Utilize hashtags to boost engagement and communication

In June 2013, Facebook linked sites like Twitter, Pinterest, and Google+ by working out the use of hashtags, which seem as clickable links in Page and personal accounts updates and in posts on the news feed. Hashtags are a process of grouping similar types of content collectively, and can be generated by typing a hash or pound symbol directly before a word while creating a status update or comment on your Page or personal account, like this: "What do you love regarding your local #walmart? Tell us utilizing the hashtag #lovewalmart and we'll pick the best to star on our site" or "It's Gap's winter sale, with up to 60% off! Come take a peek... #gapsale." where "#walmart" and "#gapsale" are clickable. Clicking on a hashtag will begin a feed where you will see stories from the Pages and people who have posted with the identical hashtag. People can utilize hashtags in Facebook search to find posts related to specific topics or concerns. Billions of parts of material are shared on Facebook each day peaking in the 8-11pm primetime slot - so hashtags provide a huge opportunity for brands and marketers to participate in conversations in a meaningful, relevant and timely way. While hashtag use hasn't blown up in the way Facebook assumed it might, used sparingly they still can be of advantage. Several techniques to use hashtags efficiently on Facebook:

- Use one or two strategic hashtags associated to your company or industry in your Facebook posts, particularly if they will be used for crossplatform promotion), e.g. #yourcompanysname. You can also use hashtags as a method to display an emotion or feeling relating to your post, e.g. #shoptillyoudrop, #excited, or #itstheweekend.

- Each Facebook Page has its own individual URL with a status update case at the top; the composition of the URL is www.facebook.com/hashtag/yourhashtag. Direct traffic to that URL from other places, e.g. your blog, other social networks, company cards, in-store purchasing materials, etc. to promote conversation.Use a URL condenser similar bit.ly to obtain the link even more memorable.

- Find new Pages and partners by seeking for specific hashtags in Facebook search, and track your own hashtags to observe what people are speaking concerning you and your company, then join the chat.

Keep your engagement timely

If a person comments on a status update you do or posts a public message on your wall, be certain to reply to it as quickly as possible. Any chance to further the discussion, answer a query, or give gratitude for a consumer's support is all but forgotten if there is no reply – and it's something a lot of companies on Facebook fail to do, to their loss. If your Page is actually busy and you simply do not have the time to reply to every fan comment, giving a "like" (rather than ignoring them) will at least show that you are hearing to what they have to tell.

Use @mentions to be personable and up engagement

When responding to individual fans' comments on your Page, practice the @username function to approach each person individually. It will add a personal touch to your assistance and make the consumer in question feel special, especially as they will receive a notification to let them know you answered. Type @ and commence typing the name of the person you desire to reply to quickly afterwards. When their name arises, select it with a mouse click or the tap of a finger. If you desire to be more informal and address a client only by their first name, place your cursor at the end of their name (after it appears in the comment box) and hit backspace a few times until their name disappears. To that end, add a individual touch to any status updates or comments you make by 'signing' with your first name. This is particularly useful if multiple admins are addressing followers on the same page.

Add Timeline milestones, utilize as marketing opportunities

Facebook enables you to add Milestones in the account of your company (past and present) on your Page by scrolling through and recording dates on your timeline (e.g. when the company was established, your 1000th sale, etc.). These assist flesh out your company history and can give consumers a fascinating insight into your growth over the months and years (particularly if you were in business way before Facebook rolled around). You can even utilize upcoming milestones as a means to connect with clients and provide them with an incentive to remain Interested.

Promote Events on Facebook–Ask followers to subscribe

Click on the Events option in the status update box to organize your event, whether they will happen offline (like a shop's opening) or online (like a live webinar or the source of a sale). Be certain to upload a photo of the event - a move that is often ignored, and also build excitement with countdown statuses recalling people to confirm their presence as the event gets nearer. When you organize an event, you can also add targeting so only the most important people will see your Page's event in their News Feeds. You're also able to target your event's invites based on standards such as gender, place and age at the bottom of the Create New Event window. Events assist promote your Page naturally because when someone RSVPs to one, it will generate a story in their friends' News Feed. To get more followers on board, post the event well in advance and regularly remind (via Page posts) that it's all taking place soon!

Use Facebook Groups to grow your business

Facebook Groups are a useful way to network with peers, strengthen relationships with current customers, or attract new ones - whether you create your own or join one of the millions that already exist. To get the most advantage from groups which concentrate on discussions regarding your chosen industry, your intention should be to position yourself as an specialist figure: be active, give assistance, and be reliable , i.e. no focus on selling. Over time, your information and influence will be identified and this will assist to stimulate people's interest, perhaps sufficient to make them want to consider your product or service. Another big opportunity for business is in local community groups that focus on buying or selling all manner of products and services; most people in built-up areas will be able to find one set up for their town or city. Find your local group, scope out how trade takes place, and offer up your wares in an appropriate manner. Alternatively, if you create your own group, it can exist as a place to provide customer support, promote upcoming events, get feedback on upcoming products, and for customers to connect, collaborate, and share (valuable consumer insight for you!). Use the group's About section to explain how the group works, and to steer the conversation and activity you would like to see.

Paid Advertising Strategy on Facebook

A budget for Facebook advertising is greatly important consideration as component of your marketing strategy, especially because the competition for eyeballs on the site's content is ever-increasing, in tandem with the site intentionally decreasing organic (non-paid) reach - especially for self-promotional Page posts. In fact, Facebook now intentionally limits the display in the News Feed of Page Post content that highlights only promotional information - asking people to buy something, urging them to enter a sweepstakes, etc., which gets paid promotion even more important. You would not launch a real-world game and expect people to just set up and continue to advance their interest without advertising, and a Facebook Page is certainly no different. Luckily, you do not need to spend a lot: Facebook advertisements can be a cheap and efficient way to get new followers, keep existing fans interested, direct people to your website, or get them to do whatever you want on the way to attaining your marketing aims. Consider this: if you designate just $1 of marketing spend per day on Facebook ads, your content will be exposed to several thousand people that would not otherwise have noticed it. If you are doing this and your rivals aren't, you'll be way leading in the information game for your company corner.

The most fundamental Facebook advertising: boosting posts

To increase the average reach of your most significant posts - like exclusive offers, prominent events, or a company milestone, Facebook supports you to utilize its "Boost Post" tool, discovered via a button under each status update. Boosted posts serve for three days and will expand the reach of your content exceeding the people who see it naturally. In basic terms, boosted posts generate a set of immediate Facebook advertisements, without any of the specific customization options accessible through the main Facebook advertisements tool. Boosted posts do the following:

- Promote your post within mobile and computer News Feeds of Followers.

- Advertise your post within mobile and desktop News Feeds of followers, their friends, and via a limited set of alternatives like age, gender, interests, and place.

- Create a Sponsored Story advertisement within mobile and computer News Feeds.

CHAPTER 5

TWITTER TIPS: TWEET YOUR WAY TO THE TOP

Twitter is used by millions of companies and individuals as a way to monitor communications about their companies, communicate with customers, manage consumer service issues, promote offers, share rich and appealing content like images and videos - all inside 140 characters per tweet. A 2013 study by analytics corporation KISS metric even discovered that Twitter users were more inclined to buy from companies they follow on the site by a perimeter of 64 percent, and that's just one statistic regarding a site that has the potential, arguably more comprehensive than any other social network, to connect with consumers and to generate loyal brand advocates. In this chapter, we will investigate some of the techniques to make this an actuality for you.

Twitter Account Setup Strategy

No stellar Twitter policy is perfect without a profile built to knock the socks off your consumers, so let's begin with some essential setup and optimization suggestions.

Top Twitter username, and a suggestion for the "Name" box

Your Twitter username is remarkably important, as it will make up section of your Twitter profile URL - the address you will put on all of your marketing stuff to direct somebody to follow you on the social network. Try to retain your username short, simplistic and memorable. Most companies use their company name as their username, so that their address shows www.twitter.com/yourbusinessname. Unlike many other sites, Twitter will enable you to change your username as many times as you desire via its Settings menu, but it's worth remembering that if you've advertised one username for a while, unexpectedly turning to a new one would not do good business judgment.

Write an appealing Twitter Bio, use

real names

Your Twitter profile is likely to rise high up in web search outcomes for your individual or company name, so it's important that you utilize its 160 character bio right (the bio text is utilized as the search link's information and, of course, arises on your Twitter profile itself). Utilize the small space to correctly and succinctly inform people who you are, what you do, and why they should follow you; practice an upbeat tone to reflect Twitter's fun and conversational environment, and if you are an individual, single "descriptor" words distributed by commas, lines, or hyphens (e.g. globetrotter | entrepreneur | whisky lover...")are commonly utilized space-savers. If you're a company, it's a great idea to enter the real name of the person managing your Twitter account so that consumers feel like more like they're communicating to a person rather than a faceless brand. If you have space, you might also desire to throw in a URL, or @mentions to link to other accounts you are connected with, and even company or industry-related hashtag, too - but be cautious that the latter does not mess up the readability and stability of the bio as a complete.

Upload an efficient Twitter profile image

Ditch the default Twitter avatar and utilize a photo of yourself or company's logo. You could even merge the two, but make sure that a face is definitely visible - Twitter's one-to-one communications mean that people will recognize much more closely with a profile that represents a person's smiling face rather than the dreaded default 'egg' image or something likewise anonymous. Twitter suggests that your profile image be uploaded at 400 x 400 pixels. To edit your header picture, click the "Edit profile" button on your page and then "Edit your profile picture."

Generate a custom Twitter header picture

In April 2014, Twitter introduced a new version of its computer profiles, full with a big 1500 x 500 pixel Facebook-esque header image - a large banner that spans the whole width of the page, ripe for customizing with your own design. Although a majority of Twitter users now access the site via mobile devices, there's certainly no harm in making sure your desktop profile captures the imagination of the still-millions of people that browse on desktops. How you select to fill the header image is up to you, but tactics similar to Facebook - simple branding, highlighting promotions, featuring customers, etc. are a few of the various common approaches. To edit your header picture, click the "Edit profile" switch on your page and then "Edit your header picture."

Create a custom Twitter background image

In previous versions of Twitter for desktop, users could upload a custom design that spanned the whole width of the profile page's background. Although this is no longer possible on the "home" page of a Twitter profile, you can still insert a background image to appear when someone clicks on an individual tweet to view it (and the conversation attached to it) on a separate page. Although the eyeballs this portion of your Twitter profile's branding will be considerably less than that your cover photo, the people that do click individual tweets are, by nature, probably more interested in what you have to say, so the background customization here might appeal to them more than the average Twitter user.

Twitter Marketing and Content Strategy

How's that Twitter account looking? Pretty good? Great! Now let's see at some content tactics to assist your company's attendance on Twitter shine bright like a diamond.

Concoct the comprehensive tweet, attach a sign off

Spelling, punctuation and syntax all count, particularly when you only have 140 characters to convey your point in a single tweet. Exercise writing the perfect tweet, and constantly double-check for mistakes. While it might be attractive to use text speak to cram as many as you can into Twitter's 140-character limit,doing so is at greatest unprofessional, and at worst creates your tweets unclear. If you have multiple tweeters on the identical account, be sure to enable space to add a 'sign off' at the conclusion of each tweet, e.g. initials like "^AM", so consumers are clear who they are communicating with. And as customers want to know who they are communicating with, why not include a picture of the people replying to users' questions in your Twitter cover design too?

Do not surpass the tweet limit

Wherever feasible, do not enable your Twitter statuses to scatter over into various tweets, as this makes it complicated for your followers to keep record of what you are trying to say, particularly if they have a really busy Twitter feed, where your updates may arrive sandwiched between tweets emerging from other people that they accompany. If there is no method that you can hold a Twitter update to 140characters or fewer, think using a applications like TwitLonger as a workaround. This application allows you to type as long a tweets as you desire. When you submit the tweet, it will be delivered to your followers using your Twitter account. The first part will be visible, then a URL will be presented to allow followers to click through to view the full message at the Twitlonger website.

Tweets: strive for quality and consistency; do not spam

Do not post tweets every minute of the day, spamming your followers' feeds and bothering them sufficient to unfollow you - be sparing. Independent investigation has shown that posting more than two or three tweets an hour can end in a decrease in commitment, while Twitter's own study found that companys' that tweet two to three times a day can normally reach an audience that is equivalent to 30% of their followers during any given week. Of course, a lot of circumstances can affect this evaluation (e.g. if one special tweet goes viral and the rest do not), and you can mark this with the site's analytics tool, but the principal stands - quality perpetually surpass quantity.

Tweet your best content numerous times, schedule for ease

Twitter does, theoretically, show people all of the tweets from people who follow an account, but the site is so dynamic and fast-moving, and people also check them at different times of the day, that your content can easily be missed. To help prevent this, do not be afraid to post the identical content under various guises, several occasions a day (i.e. practice with unique wording and separate headlines for the same article one or two hours apart, then see which wording worked best).If you create a lot of valuable "perpectual" blog content, i.e. that which will be useful no matter its age, use a service like Buffer to program and automatically post tweets connecting to this content regularly.

Share appealing content, use past victory to shape future material

To help grow your followers and build relationships with customers, share the types of selfless and engaging content including links to useful and interesting content (whether your own or by others). Utilize Google Alerts to be informed of fun, fresh, and appropriate content for your Twitter news feed and followers. If you will be adding a link to your individual material within a tweet, always shorten it before utilizing a site like bit.ly. Twitter will shrink links automatically, but utilizing bit.ly also enables you to customize them for neatness and examine the click-through rate, which is excellent for seeing what kind of content resonates completely with your followers. When using a shortened link on Twitter, double check that it operates before posting. One broken link might imply a customer never clicks on your URLs again. To compound the result of a tweet including a link, upload an image with it to assist it stand out with individual's news feeds.

Use hashtags to group tweets, drive commitment, and research

Use #hashtags to group tweets of the identical kind and to highlight your message. Top-trending hashtags surface on Twitter's home page, and can quickly be discovered via Twitter search. Tweets that involve hashtags have been established to receive twice as much commitment as those without, so their usage is vital. Do not insert more than one or two hashtags per tweet, as it can get complicated for followers; commitment with tweets that involve more than two hashtags tails off considerably, research displays. Short hashtags work best. #ilovechocolatecakeandeatiteveryday - a hashtag like this is hard to read and eats up valuable characters within your tweet. In extension, use legible formatting. Symbols do not work too well, and capitalizing words aids make hashtags a bit more straightforward, e.g. #BigSale rather than #bigsale. Here are some more significant benefits of using hashtags on Twitter and other social media:

To strengthen your company's identity

Use custom-made hashtags to reinforce your

company's identity and position, e.g. #billysburgers #BerwynIL respectively, particularly useful when new consumers click to learn more regarding you. Followers also love to show off what they are up to with companions via text, image, and video updates. If you are organizing an event or launching a new promotion, make sure these fan updates are tied together strongly by publicizing and encouraging the use of a representative hashtag before, during, and after.

Pin essential Twitter posts, utilize as marketing opportunity

If you desire to spotlight a particular tweet, you can pin it to the top of your feed for extra visibility - all subsequent posts will show below it. On the PC version of Twitter, click on the 3 little dots below a tweet and select"pin to your profile page." Utilize a pinned tweet to highlight one of your most engaged-with tweets, an essential announcement, an forthcoming event, a tweet that summarizes your brand and its mission, or a message that spurs emotion and encourages people to share and spread brand awareness through retweeting, e.g.something funny or inspirational.

Leave space to encourage tweet comments; fashion your own

As lots of people like to add their own comments to the back of someone else's tweet (when retweeted via a program like Tweetdeck, for example) or a link shared to Twitter from an external website, I recommend that manually-typed tweets and those that are auto-created when someone hits the "Tweet" button next to a blog post or item on your website) do not exceed 120 characters wherever possible. That leaves a retweeter 20 characters to add their own response. To frame this tactic as when it is you who is the tweeter or retweeter of someone's opinion or cool link you've found, you can use the remaining space to express your reaction, e.g. "Love this by @janejones!" or pose a question to your followers, e.g. "Do you ever use this strategy?"

Respond to @mentions and DMs in a regular manner, and with personality

Whenever you get notification of an @mention of your company, be certain to respond as soon as possible. Replying to a consumer or fan with a mention is a quick, easy, and hugely powerful way to make someone feel like you're really paying attention; it makes them feel happy and appreciated and, in turn, promotes positive connotations towards your business. Just think how lovely (and sometimes unexpected!) it seems to receive a quick recognition or comment from a company or personality that you like, and you will start to realize the value in this way. A lot of the bigger businesses do not reply to a large proportion of brand notices, and it hits their reliability hard. As I've harped on regarding plenty already in this book, people on social media like to join with other people.

So, try to apply in some brand personality to your responses where you can, utilizing your tone of voice and communicating the person by name. It's a magnificent way to bring company accounts to life and absolutely connect with the consumer. To go that extra mile where the position calls for it, a follow-up tweet like a simple "Everything still good?" is a fantastic way to ensure that a customer's issue is truly resolved.

Search and get clients from the rivals

If you have a local rival, search for tweets discussing their company name as well as your own. I would not wholeheartedly support replying to the tweets you

84

encounter, because it could come across as too being too hopeless or forward, but just understanding what is being said about your opponent can be enough to give you approaches to assist you up your own game and give you a aggressive edge. If you do determine to answer to tweets considering your rivals (if the rival firm does not ever reply, for instance), be helpful and conversational with no put-downs and no hard selling. Surely your good grace will prepare the consumer in question to switch loyalties.

Thank your latest followers

When someone follows you, be certain to @reply to thank them if you have the time, or retweet something exciting from their feed - it's a great icebreaker at the commencement of what, probably, will be a long relationship. Don't be motivated to use a device to auto-thank users who follow, or send them promotional stuff. As a first impression, it does not go down well at all. I normally say something like this to initiate discussion: "Hey, @newfollower, thanks for following! How are you doing today? Andrew."

Paid Advertising on Twitter

While Twitter advertising does not have the same excellent depth as Facebook's tools, it can yet be a very powerful approach in assisting you reach an extended audience through your tweets. To start setting up a Twitter ad operations, click Twitter advertisements from the drop-down menu on your account or visit https://ads.twitter.com/ and click the "Create new campaign" badge. There are five main Twitter advertisement products to select from, depending on what aim you desire to accomplish:

Followers (Promoted Account): Apply simple copy that explicitly tells people what you desire them to do (follow you!), and spell out the advantages - receiving deals and discounts, private news, etc. Refrain from attaching links or pictures that will withdraw from that most important "Follow" button. With advanced accounts, your Twitter username, profile picture and a Follow button will also arrive as a suggestion in vital spots across Twitter on PC and mobile, such as the Who to Follow box and Home timelines. If utilizing this choice, ensure that your profile image, name, and bio are in tip-top appearance, as this, in enhancement to your copy, is what people will be operating upon.

Website clicks or conversions: Combine this possibility with a Website Card for greater influence. Unlike an average tweet that may just represent a plain link, Website Cards give a preview photo and extra information about your site. The intention is that the eye-catching arrangement of these tweets (complete with image, text caption, story headline and call to action button, e.g. "Read more...") will enable you to easily surface website material within a tweet and encourage consistent traffic to your home page, commodity page, or an essential blog post.

Tweet engagements: Use this opportunity to encourage higher levels of action on your Twitter posts; particularly important to generating buzz around something like a product launch, upcoming event, or seasonal occasion.

App installs or engagements: encourage people to install your mobile app. Users can open or install the app directly within your tweet which will, of course, tell people why they can't live without your offering.

Leads on Twitter: Use this option if you're looking to grow your email list

subscribers, and combine it with a lead generation card. Offer potential sign-ups something valuable in return for their email address (prize draw entry, free download, etc.). Persuasive language like "get", "win" and "receive" can often be used to inspire action.

CHAPTER 6
INSTAGRAM TIPS:SNAP-HAPPY MARKETING STRATEGY

Instagram, the fun and quirky picture app, has taken the globe by storm since starting in October 2010. Hundreds of millions of individuals utilize Instagram as a way to change everyday photos and videos with filters and frames, into memory-laden material, which can then be shared with the universe. Chances are that pictures and videos of your company are already on Instagram, and all of this material acts as genuine peer-to-peer endorsements of you - basically free advertising. With a sound approach of your own, you can only assist to compound this effect, increasing brand loyalty and encouraging sales as a result. Some have even called Instagram "The World's Most Influential Selling Tool," such is the level of emotion its users show. They are young, they are involved, and many of them are Shoppers.

Understand the "Culture of Instagram"

The top-performing companies on Instagram all have 1 thing in common: they know what makes the application different compared to other social networks, and utilize this information to their advantage. While the meaning of "Instagram culture" will surely change over time, at its heart are users who are satisfied of the content they post - you won't see numbers of spontaneous selfies and blurry night club pictures from the most popular "artists", for example. As such, there is a clear lean towards quality over volume, which sees producers taking their time to correctly compose and create photos and videos, cropping and editing continuously they are just right so that when an object does ultimately get posted to their Instagram feed, it is streamed over by fascinated followers, complemented with loads of likes and comments, and brings new fans ("Wow, these guys post exceptional stuff and get a lot of love; I'm staying around for more!") in the method. One of Instagram's fundamental mantras is to support people to "find beauty everywhere." For companies, this implies showing how your company sees the society, sharing imagery that drives people's opinions of you deeper than the common knowledge, and offering a picture into the lifestyle that your commodity or service makes potential both through your own eyes and those of consumers who utilize them. In short, whereas visual imagery for situations like Facebook and Twitter might seldom be more ad-hoc in nature or Pinterest more simple and mood board, your preference on Instagram should be more productive, arty, and special, with even more of an emphasis on visible storytelling, turning ordinary circumstances into artistic moments, and seizing the essence of your company throughout. Submerge yourself in the culture of Instagram by reflecting this more imaginative style of photos or videos in your own feed (clearly expressing a defined personality and voice and mirroring the attitude and preferences of app's majority audience), and you'll be in a significantly dominant situation from the get go.

What are the components of a top quality Instagram picture?

As you now know, posting any past photo onto Instagram just won't cut it with the app's savvy viewers; you have to be much more creative and selective. One of the greatest ways to determine what kinds of photos

Instagram actually requires companies to post in order to keep followers content is to look at its proposals for Instagram ads:

- No massive use of image filters as a way to hide the "reality" of a shot, and no text overlays are provided.

- Companies can not feature their logo in Instagram advertisements other than as a natural, non-obvious part of the picture.

- Images used as advertisements must be "true to your company", i.e. not offensive or cheesy, and no use of gimmicks.

- Photos utilized for ads should seize "moments", not outcomes. In other words, advertisements must not just be a shot of your product, but something more productive and inspiring.

- Advertisements should practice ideas and take cues from the existing Instagram society, particularly from famous hashtags.

As you read through the remainder of the advice in the chapter, keep these thoughts in the back of your consciousness as you think regarding how you desire to develop your own Instagram approach. As with a lot of social media applications, they won't implement to every situation all of the time, but as a good reason for your activity? Pretty great stuff.

Optimize your Instagram bio, add a profile picture that fits a circle

One of the simplest ways to join with would-be Instagram followers is to optimize your bio. Use the entire 150 characters allowed to assist followers: give them a goal to follow you, tell them what gives you unique, remind somebody that they will be amongst the first to know about special offers and advertisements, first to get a sneak peek at new commodity lines, and have the first opportunities to enter Instagram competitions to win stuff! Do not overlook adding the URL to your website in your bio section too – the only spot on Instagram where a link will be immediately clickable. Keep the mood light and fun, include important keywords (for SEO), an Emoji if the state fits, and a business-specific hashtag. Interestingly, many organizations are deliberately choosing to include a link to their blog instead of a web store, showing how they see Instagram as an opportunity to slowly build their brand image as a whole, rather than "force" people into buying right away.

Equally as essential is to add a photo or profile yourself if you're the figurehead of your company (ideally of your smiley face) or, instead, your company logo, as this will represent you all across the service Like Google+, Instagram (on its mobile app at least) supports a circular profile photo, which suits looks better than it does business logos. If your logo is square and badly cropped when you upload it to your Instagram profile, use my square-logo-into-circle-fit template as an simple fix.

Only post your best pictures, find motivation from other users

The best companies on Instagram are remarkably picky regarding the photographs they post on their accounts - unlike any other social networks (e.g. a gallery of photos of an event you'd post to Facebook), quality clearly trumps quantity where your portfolio is involved. Take your time in creating a number of photos that you are really pleased of - your very best efforts - as it is this that will reach the eye of users both when observed as unique pieces of content, and when your gallery is surveyed through as a whole. Many of the biggest companies on Instagram post just once per day, sometimes they do not even post. Here are some basic picture-taking tips and guidelines that will assist to lift the quality of your business on Instagram:

1. View the universe in squares (but don't fret regarding it too much)

Traditionally, pictures on Instagram have been squares - like an old Polaroid picture – and this persists the most common type of presentation on the social network. So before the shutter shuts on your bigscreen camera scene, try and imagine how your story might appear as a square once the sides are cropped. However, if there is a significant element of your content that a square will frustratingly crop out, you will be comforted to know that Instagram, in August 2015, added the capability to publish photos and videos in portrait and landscape mode. When uploading material, just tap the format icon to select the orientation.

2. The rule of thirds

Just with other forms of photography, the 'rule of

thirds' is strongly rooted in several of the great Instagram shots. Visualize your viewfinder is divided into thirds, both horizontally and vertically (or turn on the iPhone Camera grid view via Options); now balance your composition between these areas.

3. Get symmetrical

Symmetrical pictures look great with Instagram. You will finish with a comprehensive square crop of your picture. When taking your photo, the solution is to center yourself absolutely and make certain all your lines are dead accurate.

4. Play with angles and lines

Instagram is all regarding encouraging its users to view the world in a new fashion. We are all so habitual to seeing the world from head height, so experiment with high and low angles, from behind, or at the side, to add interest and intrigue to your snaps. In addition, think regarding including lines into your photos - natural ingredients like a line or trees or a road extending into the distance - to draw somebody's eyes into the picture, or towards whatever it is you desire them to concentrate on.

5. Zoom in on details

To make the most of the comparatively small real estate of mobile devices (where most people will be viewing your Instagram content), make a habit of focusing in on particular details of products or service in order to draw customers in, rather than blander long or mid-range shots. For instance, a clothing store might highlight the quality dye and material in a garment, while a decorating service could go a bit more abstract and use the close-up shot of a pot of paint and a brush to represent a job well done.

Brand your pictures with regular filters and image editing

Instagram's following blew up, in part, due to the facility at which users can change ordinary pictures with its vintage filters. While these overlays inhabit central to the application's appeal, over the years, its image editing tools - in reply to competition - have developed to include a description of additional benefits for photo tweaking, including straightening, lux, brightness, contrast, tilt shift, sharpening, and more. Instagram
98

enables you to set the strength of each adjustment with a simple slider. Overall, I would suggest applying them in a way that is subtle (to align with Instagram's preferred approach for brands, i.e. natural), and decide on a filter that you will use consistently; one that helps image to reflect your company's culture and personality (e.g. fun, playful, serious, professional, etc.) and make your style immediately identifiable within the feed of fans. In order to build a distinctive branded account on Instagram, discover what your followers like about you, and consistently create content around that theme; filters can play a large part in this.

Instagram Marketing and Content Strategy
Make the most of the photo caption

The photo caption that accompanies each image on Instagram subsists as a small but significant part of your marketing tactic - never leave it blank. Use it as a means to anchor the content of the image, and to exhibit your brand's character and expression of voice. Examples of applications for the photo caption entail adding a description of the goods you are featuring, asking a question or beginning a dialogue and adding a call to action or adding a URL that you need fans to visit. URLs written inside Instagram descriptions cannot be clicked on, so make sure that they are compact and exciting, utilizing a service like bit.ly to help this if required. Linked to this point, another general strategy to encourage click-throughs from Instagram captions to an address of your choice is to incorporate a phrase like "click the link in our bio." Your bio is always merely one tap away, and because the "Website" URL there is active, it will spare people the time and trouble of opening up a separate browser and typing in a URL, if that is their decision.

Instagram captions do not have a character limitation. Some companies, like National Geographic, utilize this to make every caption read like a mini-magazine article. It's a tactic that, combined with high-quality images, keeps viewers immersed in their content for longer, seeing them more than throwaway snapshots. Require to edit a caption for typographical errors or further detail? Tap the "..." icon next to your photo and select"Edit."

Double-tap to like strategy

When you scroll through the Instagram feed on your mobile phone, you can instantly and simply 'like' a picture by double-tapping it; a white heart symbol will pop up to let you know it worked. To unlike a photo, double-tap repeatedly. Inspire fans to use this way to simply 'like' your content. One year, Coca-Cola adopted the motto "Double-tap to unwrap" alongside a packaged Christmas gift as a means to inspire fans to engage. When the photo hit a set number of likes, Coca-Cola unveiled the hidden gift. You can use the very tactic as a way to "unlock" special offers or price discounts on your goods or services.

Hashtag your content, but don't be spammy; jump on trends

Using #hashtags in your Instagram captions will have the content placed with other photos with the same hashtag and turned into clickable links to see said photosets. People utilize hashtags to seek content on Instagram, so utilizing the right hashtags can assist in putting your content in front of people searching for keywords and phrases associated with your business (words in your description that are not preceded with a hashtag will not be taken into account when a user searches). Make it simple for users to find you by ensuring that your hashtag describes your content.

General hashtags like #clothes or #food might find you a few followers, but they're widely used, and your content will get lost within searches for them, so utilizing more specific and descriptive will provide a much better chance of being found and followed. Alternatively, whole Instagram communities can be built around one actionable, custom-made hashtag - and it's a tactic that works across social networks. Use the company-related hashtag you invent to bring customers together, encourage them to use it, and reward them with likes and comments when they do.

Also, study the most-used hashtags within your business niche and incorporate them into your strategy and consider taking advantage of simplified, but not overdone, hashtag trends on Instagram to help shape your content. A few examples of some of these include #thingsorganizedneatly (a top-down photo of several related items, e.g. a full outfit or multi-piece toolset, organized in a manner that is pleasing to the eye; often compounded by a use of complementary colors), #fromwhereistand (first-person, top-down shot of a person's feet, with an emphasis on footwear and the ground below in order to tell a story), #onthetable (elegant top-down photos of items on tables, particularly food), and #symmetrysundays (marking the end of the week with an eye-catching symmetrical scene from your store, city, or elsewhere).

The power of geotagging on Instagram (and a little trick)

Instagram allows you to geotag your photos with the location at which they were taken, which are then added to a Photo Map. When a picture is tagged in this way, Instagrammers who are close to your location or who visit it at a later date will be able to view your photos. The resulting affinity may lead to a follow or a visit to your store, and generally adds a greater sense of place and interest to the snap. On a related note, if your business' aim is to target an audience within a specific geographic area, then the Places search tab can help you do that. As well as providing you the opportunity to engage with the Top and Most Recent posts from any location, use what you see as inspiration for publishing the type of content popular with people in a specific area. A stunning landscape shot, a unique take on a famous landmark, a subtle nod to your business and what it offers, etc.

Instagram contest strategy

Instagram contests are hugely familiar and can provide a swift, affordable, and powerful way to inspire fans to engage with your brand, and spread the word regarding you across Instagram and ahead. Here is a sequence of simple measures to help guarantee your Instagram contest is a success:

1. **Choose a prize:** Pick a reward that is unique to your business, e.g., a product or gift card so that you will draw entrants who are genuinely interested in your business, not just in winning an iPad or $300 cash, for example. Try to make the size of the reward proportionate to the energy it will take to accomplish it.

2. **Decide on an entrance method:** Some of the most simplistic contest entry methods on Instagram involve asking followers to like a photo, follow your account, or re-post a photo (with an application like Regram or merely screengrabbing your published photo). You can also choose to promote a contest held elsewhere, like on your Facebook Page or your website, through your Instagram account, and encourage people to those addresses via a memorable shortened URL in your image's caption or a clickable link in your Instagram bio. Other than that, some of the most popular entry methods require users to post a photo or a video on

Instagram to be enrolled; often tied to a distinct theme, e.g., food, seasons, colors and their favorite product from your range.

3. **Build your contest:** When you begin the contest with a post on Instagram, emphasizing an attention-grabbing title with a brief call-to-action will help to maximize entries, e.g., "Register to Win a $100 Gift Card from Sean's Salon!" A photo of the award is an excellent way to entice people to register to win it. If you are giving away a gift card, for instance, insert an image with the gift card value in text and a product that people can purchase with it. Write the entry process and prizing information in the description - a section with information about the award, how to register and any rules or limitations for your contest, associated with a short URL or a clickable link in your bio.

4. **Monitor progress:** To help assess the progress of your Instagram contest:

   - Use hashtags to efficiently track how many pictures are being shared on Instagram that have your contest hashtag (urge fans to use one in the caption for the photos or videos they share as a condition for entry, but make sure beforehand that your preferred hashtag is uncommon and hasn't been utilized by someone else before).

- Set up Google Alerts to observe mentions of your contest over the web.

- Use Wishpond or Woobox Instagram contest web applications for real-time operations reports, which enables you to track views, entries, and growth rates.

5. **Promote your contest:** In addition to general marketing of your competition, post an email to your mailing record (these are the people most inclined to subscribe), advertise your contest on social networks, and add a banner to the home page of your website. You may also choose to stream competition entries to your website or a custom tab on your Facebook Page based on a particular @mention or hashtag, to assist spread the word - the latter can be accomplished via a service like Woobox.

6. **Follow-up actions:** After your competition is over, follow these measures to wrap everything up correctly:

- Showcase winning photos on your Instagram story and other social channels.

- Share a video showing you picking the winning photo to generate excitement.

- Post teasers for anticipated contests on Instagram to maintain your fans hooked, keep the energy going, and prime fans for future competitions on your Instagram account.

- Run weekly contests on Instagram to get fans into the attitude of looking forward to them and registering.

Embed your Instagram photos and videos

When you see an Instagram picture or video on your desktop web browser, you will see a share button on the right-hand side (just below the comments button). Click this button, and you will get an embed code that you can copy and paste into your website, blog, or article. Handily, the embedded image or highlights an Instagram logo, when clicked, will take viewers to your Instagram profile where they can find more of your content.

Instagram video enhancement

Instagram video's editing and improvement options are elementary at best, but there exists a whole class of apps to add a bit of style and distinctiveness to your mobile video efforts - if your video creation exists outside of the Instagram applications, that is. Some of my preferences include iMovie, Videohance (iOS), and Vidtrim (Android). The Flipagram application can also be utilized to stitch various photos together to produce a story-driven slideshow video.

Target your most committed followers by location and demographics

As you can DM up to 15 people personally via Instagram Direct, you can use this as an chance to segment and target your viewers based on area. To track down your most committed followers, survey through your photostream for the people who most comment and like your content, or regularly tag their friends as a means to increase awareness of your brand. Once you've recognized your most enthusiastic fans, you can form different group messages to send to multiple segments of your viewers. Use these as a means to share news on new goods, announce giveaways and contests, administer Q&A sessions, push traffic to your website, and more. Of course, since these messages will be frequently unsolicited, you should be very positive, and extra cautious, that sending them will not bother people who are most inclined to be your biggest brand ambassadors.

Give ultra-exclusive sneak peeks

In a pretty savvy move and one you can imitate - Kardashian Kollection offered 15 of its followers an exclusive behind the scenes photo from its latest fashion collection. To enter, Instagram followers were asked to screengrab the image which informed them of the entry guidance and re-post it with the hashtag #KKDIRECT. The promotion gained over 7,000 likes and 800 comments in under 24 hours… and the smart part? By asking followers to re-post the entry instructions, they put their followers to work in assisting to drive more members. After the promotion, screengrabs of the private messages being sent to the elected 15 were posted publically for transparency.

Instagram ads best practice

As you should now be well knowledgeable, Instagram is a community where people go to discover and become motivated by the images they see. The best methods for ads reflect much of what you have discovered about content marketing on Instagram so far – make ads seamless to the action, not disruptive. As a business, it is suggested that you concentrate your Instagram ad operations around three principal objectives: on-brand, concept-driven, and well crafted.

1. **On brand**

   Like regular Instagram content, your ads should be artistic, showing your brand's character. Find unique ways to include your brand's logo, icon, or color, but stay harmonious with your style within organic and paid content to drive awareness.

2. **Concept driven**

   When designing your Instagram ad, know what you want to make your viewers think and believe, and what essence of your message is. With that, you'll find it simpler to implement some of the following approaches:

- Tell a story: Take a list of images that tell a narrative about your brand and distribute them over some time.

- Experiment with visual styles: Use various filters and color schemes to create a visible mood with your images. You could also use a series of various filters to show a shift in attitude.

- Develop a theme: Create a set of unique pictures that all share a standard theme, e.g., different stories from a particular day or an object in a mixture of settings.

3. **Well crafted**

With a minimum practice, anyone can create compelling pictures for Instagram – ads or not. Here are some ad-specific suggestions.

- **Strong Focal Point:** Evade making your pictures too complex or busy. Rather, concentrate on one or two areas where you want to draw people's eyes. As a best method, one focal point should include a brand logo or another brand element that's recognizable to your viewers.

- **Framing & Balance:** Level out images to make them look more precise and consider symmetry, the rule-of-thirds, and other planning basics as you are snapping or shooting.

- **Lighting & Detail:** Be sure to use sharp and high-resolution photographs. Pixelated pictures and those with bad illumination or other defects may not work well.

- **Caption and hashtags:** Don't overlook a compelling tagline and, essential for Instagram, a choice of on-brand, and related hashtags.

- **Ad guidelines:** To evade your Instagram ads being flagged up and refused, follow the Facebook Advertising Policies, including the 20% text rule. You can monitor to make sure your picture doesn't have 20% or more of its pixels assigned to text, by using the grid tool to verify your photos.

CONCLUSION

Social Media marketing is necessary if you want your business to survive online, let alone grow, but that doesn't mean that this process needs to be super hectic. These practical marketing tips and strategies which I went through in this book can assist you to actively boost your business so you can get the most out of any resources that you have handy.

I've personally used each of these approaches to get my business off the ground when it was brand-new, and I was pretty much broke so that I can speak for their effectiveness. Back these tips up with excellent goods or services, and you'll see massive growth before you even know it.

I hope that this book helped you in getting a better understanding of the marketing and sales strategies of the Social Media World and I sincerely hope that you employ these strategies so that your businesses flourish in the best possible way and you get to achieve the heights of success that you never even had imagined of.